ANTS

ASHLEY GISH

NORTH AMERICA
EUROPE
ASIA
AFRICA
SOUTH AMERICA
AUSTRALIA

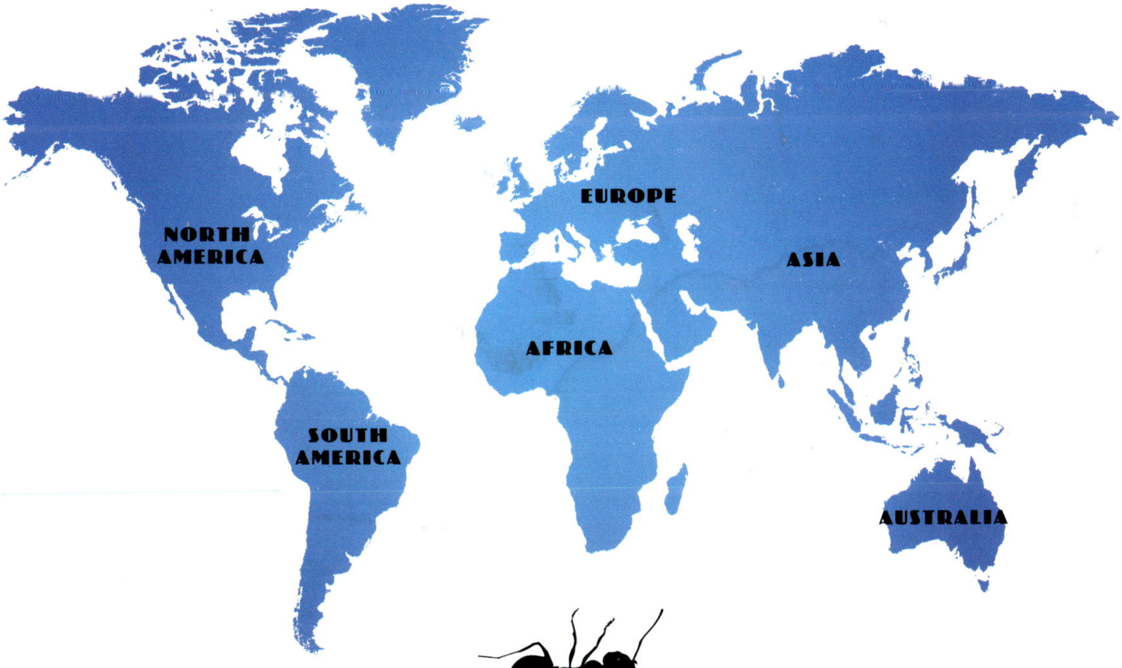

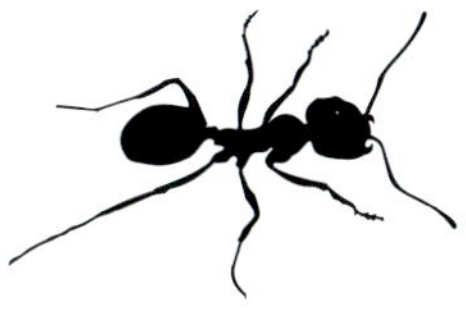

CREATIVE EDUCATION · CREATIVE PAPERBACKS

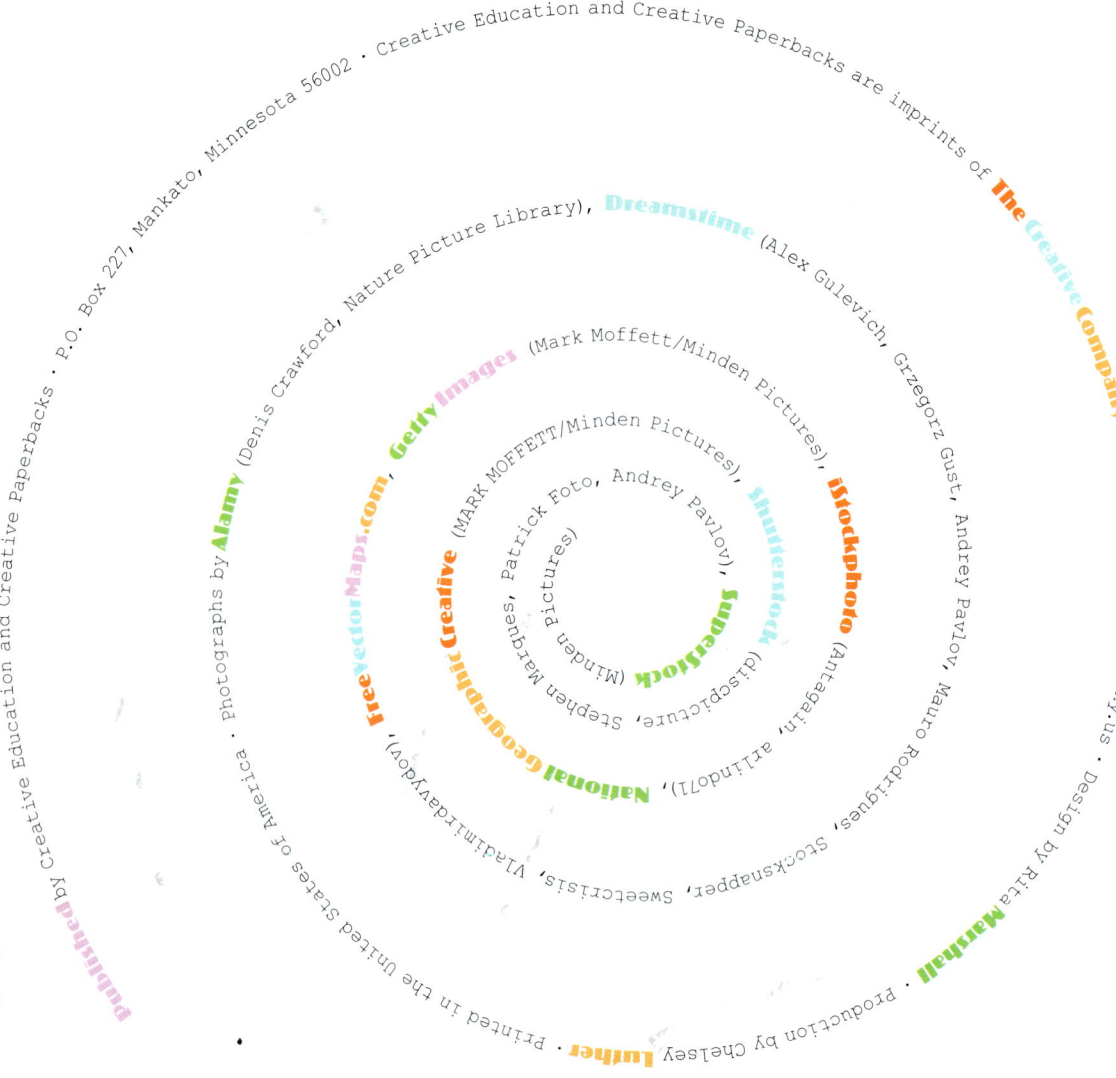

Copyright © 2019 Creative Education, Creative Paperbacks • International copyright reserved in all countries. No part of this book may be reproduced in any form without written permission from the publisher. • Library of Congress Cataloging-in-Publication Data • Names: Gish, Ashley, author. • Title: Ants / Ashley Gish. • Series: X-Books: Insects. • Includes bibliographical references and index. • Summary: A countdown of five of the most fascinating ants provides thrills as readers learn about the biological, social, and hunting characteristics of these hairy, biting insects. • Identifiers: LCCN 2017060035 ISBN 978-1-60818-987-8 (hardcover) / ISBN 978-1-62832-614-7 (pbk) / ISBN 978-1-64000-088-9 (eBook) Subjects: LCSH: 1. Ants—Juvenile literature. 2. Ants—Behavior—Juvenile literature. 3. Ant communities—Juvenile literature. • Classification: LCC QL568.F7 G4275 2018 / DDC 595.79/6—dc23
CCSS: RI.3.1-8; RI.4.1-5, 7; RI.5.1-3, 8; RI.6.1-2, 4, 7; RH.6-8.3-8
First Edition HC 9 8 7 6 5 4 3 2 1 • First Edition PBK 9 8 7 6 5 4 3 2 1

ANTS!

CONTENTS

Xceptional **INSECTS 5**

Xciting **FACTS 28**

Xtreme **TOP 5 ANTS**
#5 **10**
#4 **16**
#3 **22**
#2 **26**
#1 **31**

Xasperating **CONFLICT 24**

Xtraordinary **LIFESTYLE 18**

Xemplary **SKILLS 20**

GLOSSARY
RESOURCES
INDEX 32

XCEPTIONAL INSECTS

There are more than 12,000 kinds of ants. Some ants are soldiers. Others are workers. But queen ants rule them all in a colony. Ants' unique lifestyle makes them extreme insects.

Ant Basics

Ants are insects. They have three body parts. These are the head, thorax, and abdomen. They also have six legs and two **antennae**. They use these to explore their surroundings. **Compound eyes** allow them to hunt for food. Ant bodies are protected by an exoskeleton. They do not have bones inside their bodies like people do.

Ants use an **organ** in their abdomen to communicate with other ants. It creates scent trails. Other ants learn where to find food by following these trails.

ANTS OF THE WORLD

Ants can be found all around the world, except in the Arctic Circle and Antarctica.

GIANT AMAZONIAN ANTS

are named for their habitat. Some of the world's biggest ants, they can grow to 1.6 inches (4.1 cm).

1.6 inches (4.1 cm)

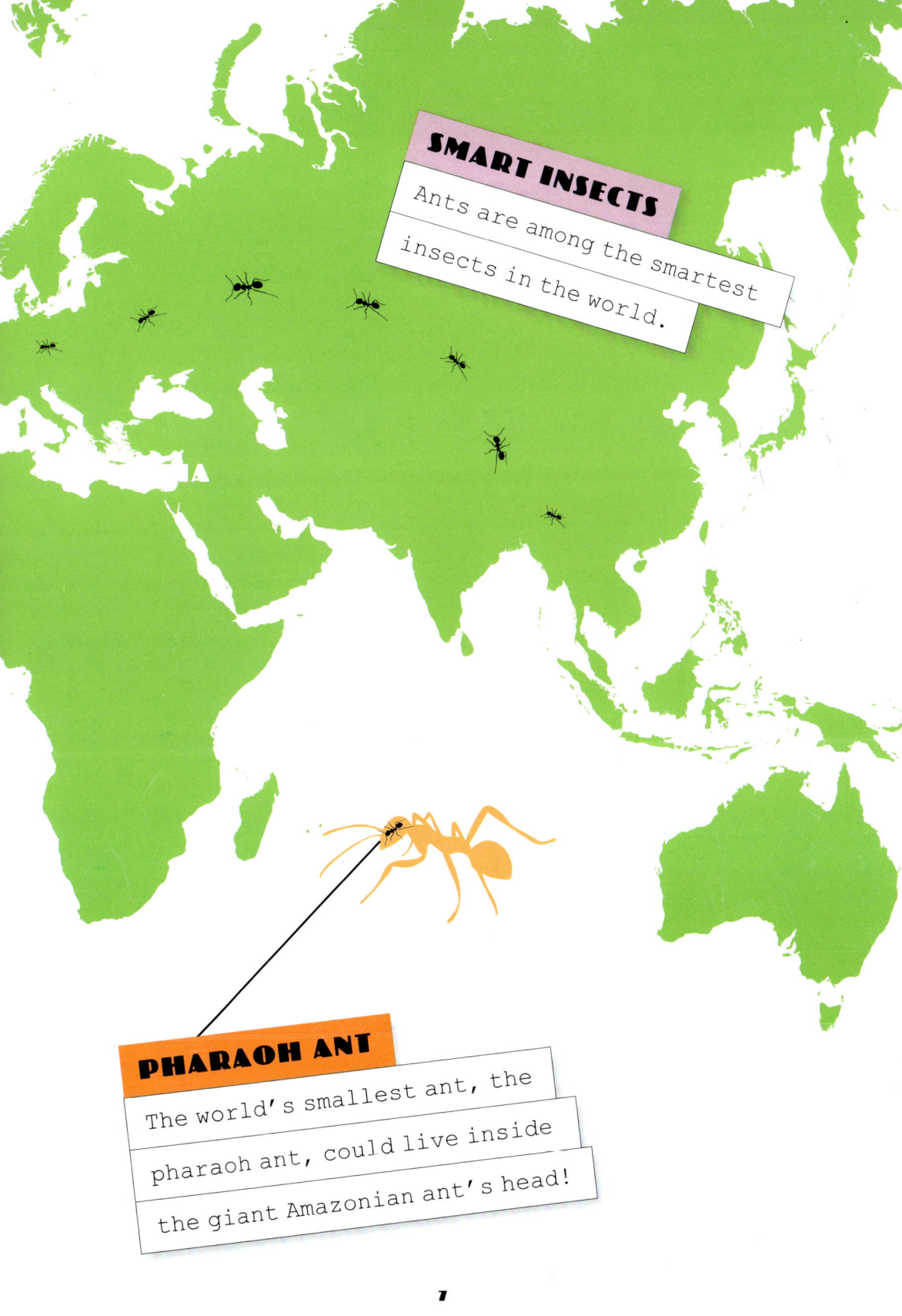

SMART INSECTS

Ants are among the smartest insects in the world.

PHARAOH ANT

The world's smallest ant, the pharaoh ant, could live inside the giant Amazonian ant's head!

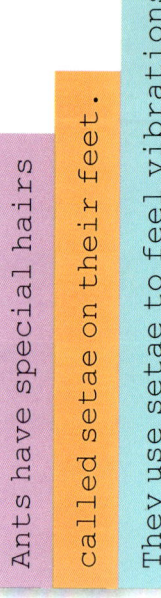

Ants have special hairs called setae on their feet. They use setae to feel vibrations.

ANTS HAVE HAIR

All ants can bite. Their mouthparts are called mandibles. Ants eat a variety of foods. But many ants eat **honeydew**. It is created by smaller insects called aphids. Army ants eat other insects, spiders, and small animals. Leafcutter ants grow their own food. First, they collect leaves. Then, they plant fungus on the leaves. Finally, the ants harvest the fungus for food.

Scientists who study ants are myrmecologists.

ANT BASICS FACT

The trap-jaw ant's mandibles snap shut faster than the blink of an eye!

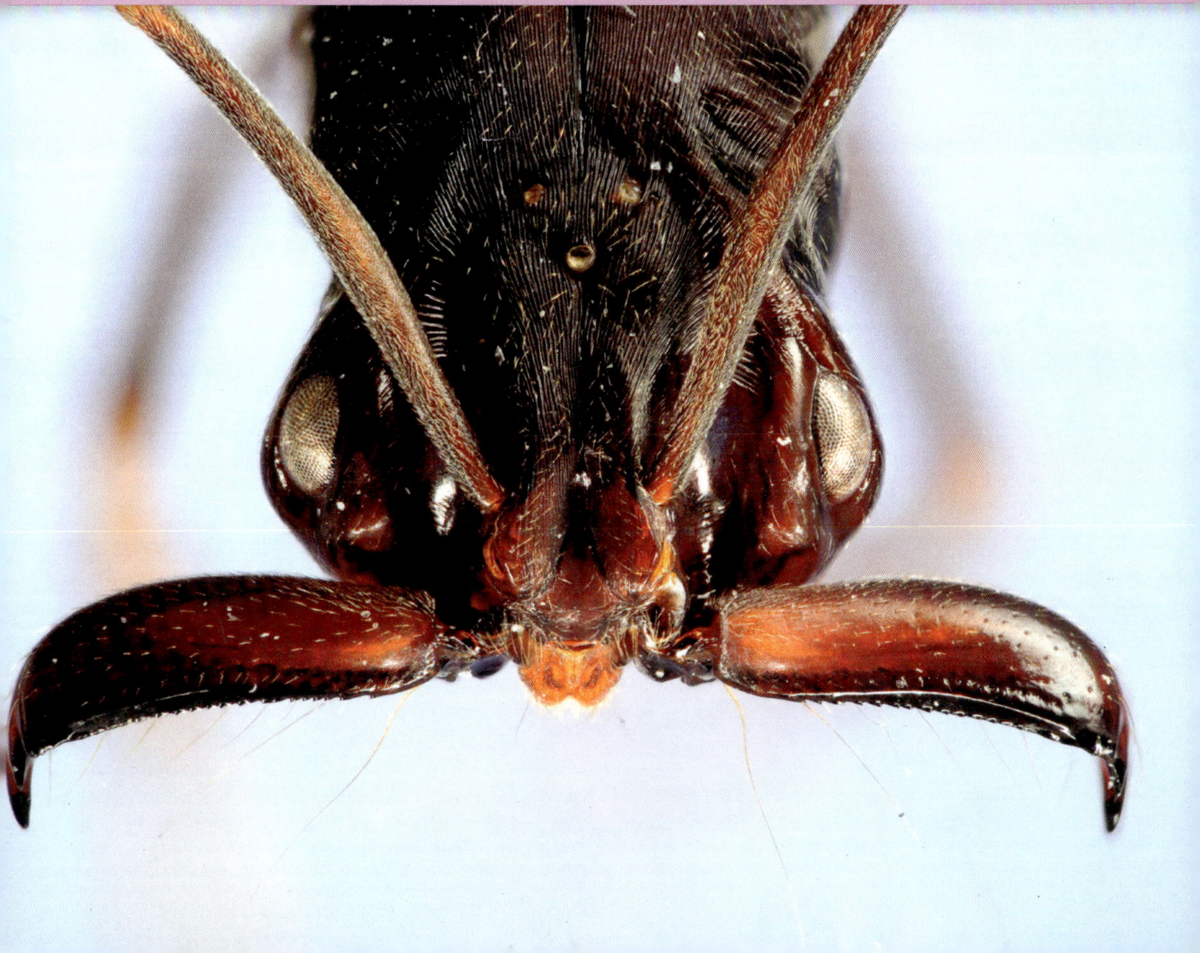

TOP FIVE XTREME ANTS

Xtreme Ant #5

Biggest Colony Argentine ants have created the largest ant colony in the world. In Europe, one colony stretches more than 3,700 miles (5,955 km). Most Argentine ants are friendly with each other. This means that one colony will not attack another. However, these ants will attack other types of ants and insects. They can wipe out termite and hornet nests quickly. In California, Argentine ants even attack horned lizards!

Ant Babies

Ants live in groups called colonies. Most colonies are led by a queen ant. Ants hatch from eggs laid by the queen. Some colonies cannot survive if the queen dies. Without her, new ants cannot be hatched. Other colonies have multiple queens. They can continue to thrive, even if one queen dies.

Ants develop through metamorphosis. This means their bodies change forms as they grow. When ants hatch from eggs, they are called larvae. Larvae do not have eyes or legs. They look like grains of rice. Worker ants feed them.

After a while, the larvae stop eating and start to grow legs. During this stage, they are called pupae. They look like adults, but their legs and antennae are folded in. The black garden ants' larvae spin cocoons. These protect the pupae while they grow.

Between 6 and 10 weeks after hatching, pupae become adult ants. Adults can be female or male. Female ants can live for many years as workers. Male ants die soon after they reproduce.

12 to **28,000** eggs laid daily

most eggs are **1** mm (.04 inch) long

2.5+ weeks

Ant queens lay eggs | The eggs hatch | Larvae eat

7 days

| 6 weeks | 10 weeks | | worker ants 7 years | queen ants 15+ years |

Pupae grow | Adults reproduce and die

male ants
3 weeks

ANT BABIES FACT

Brand-new queens are called princess ants.

They leave the nest to form their own colonies.

TOP FIVE XTREME ANTS

Xtreme Ant #4

Ant Pirates Blood-red and Amazon ants are the pirates of the ant world. Once the queen ant is ready to lay her eggs, she invades the nest of other ants. She kills the adults but cares for the eggs and larvae. This is because she will use them as slaves after they hatch. Her workers are called slave-makers. They attack other ant colonies to gather more slaves!

XTRAORDINARY
LIFESTYLE

Each ant colony has at least one queen. Ants are loyal to their queens. To us, their loyalty can appear extreme. When ants invade people's homes, conflict results.

ANT SOCIETY FACT

Ants have two stomachs.

The "social stomach" is used to feed other ants in the colony.

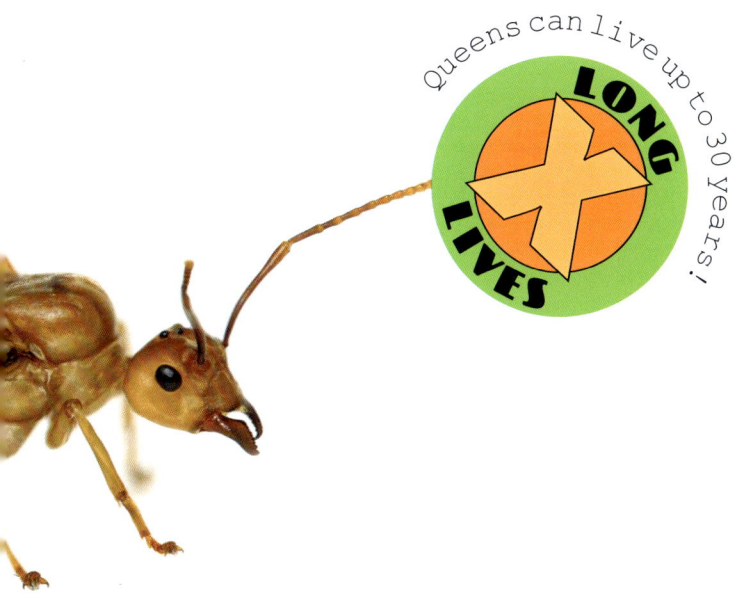

Queens can live up to 30 years!
LONG LIVES

Ant Society

Each ant has a specific job in the colony. Some ants are workers. Other ants are soldiers. Both workers and soldiers are female. Males, called drones, mate with queens to produce new queens and other females. (Male ants come from unfertilized eggs.)

Workers and soldiers are not allowed to lay eggs. If a non-queen ant tries to reproduce, she is surrounded by her sisters. They hold her down and prevent her from laying eggs.

Ants live in many different environments. Carpenter ant colonies build nests in rotten wood. Fire ants nest in tunnel systems underground. Army ants do not build nests at all. They are always on the move.

XEMPLARY SKILLS

Ants use their extreme abilities to protect themselves and their colonies. The common American field ant can lift 350 times its weight with its head. This is like a 70-pound (31.8 kg) child lifting 2 African elephants!

XEMPLARY SKILLS FACT

Most ants can hold their breath underwater for nearly 24 hours.

Every 25 days, the African driver ant queen lays up to 4 million eggs! Driver ant colonies may have up to 20 million ants. This many ants can kill a cow!

One type of carpenter ant has special muscles. It can flex these muscles in response to an attack. But flexing these muscles causes the ant to explode! The ant's explosion sprays a gluey liquid onto the attacker and slowly kills it.

Turtle ants' heads are shaped like a turtle shell or dinner plate. They use their heads to block their nest entrances. Some turtle ants can even glide through the air because of their unique body shape!

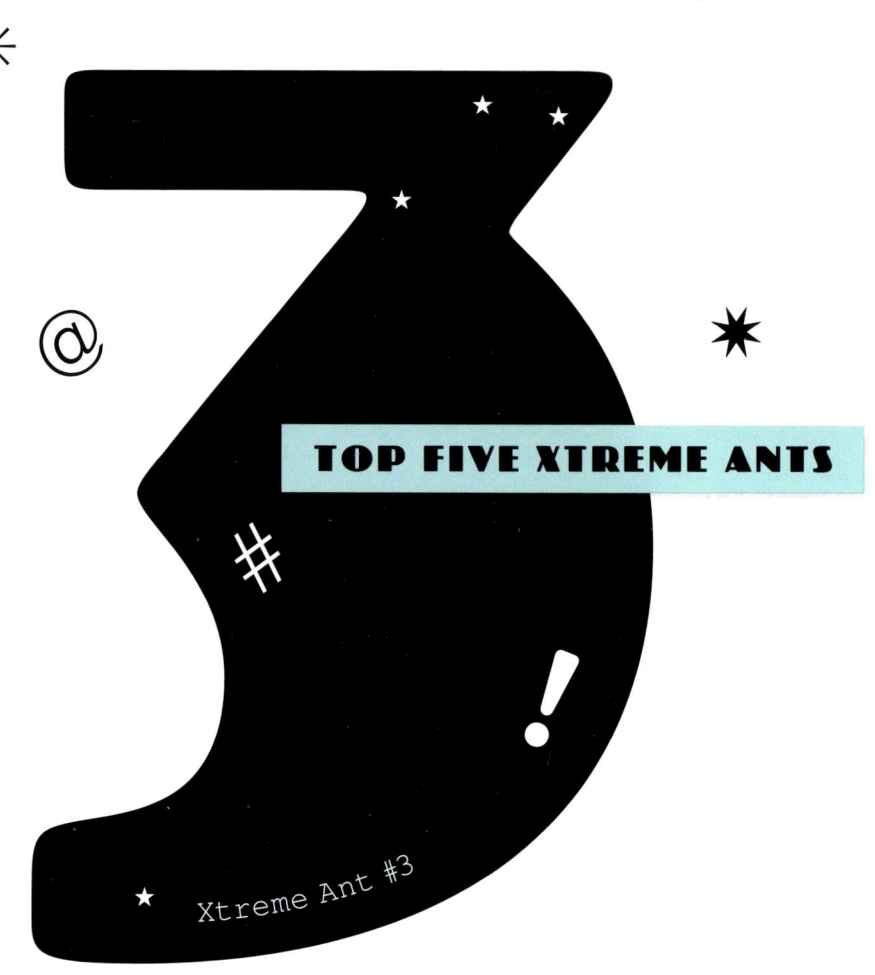

TOP FIVE XTREME ANTS

Xtreme Ant #3

Extreme Teamwork Weaver ants work as a team to build their nests. The nests are made from living leaves. The ants hold each other's feet until a long chain is formed. Then the ant at the end of the chain grabs a leaf, pulling it into position. Weaver ant larvae create the silk used to hold the nest together. Adult ants use the larvae like glue sticks. The finished nest can be as big as a soccer ball!

XASPERATING
CONFLICT

Some people see ants as beneficial. Ants that burrow into dirt introduce air to the soil. Some ants eat insects that damage crops. But sometimes, conflicts arise between ants and humans.

Ant Survival

Some people value ants for their extreme abilities. Members of the Mawé tribe in South America allow bullet ants to sting them. The bullet ant has the most painful sting in the world. Tolerating that sting is a test of manhood.

Carpenter ants are some of the most commonly seen ants in people's homes. These ants can cause problems for homeowners. They tunnel into anything made of wood.

Australia's dinosaur ant feeds at night when it is cool. If the temperature is above 41 °F (5 °C), the ants will not leave their nest. The warming climate keeps the ants from looking for food. This has caused them to become **endangered**.

As early as A.D. 304, Chinese farmers used weaver ants to protect their citrus orchards from other insects.

Besides humans, ants are the only animals that keep livestock—aphids! Lemon ant workers gather up aphids. Then the aphids can't fly away. The worker ants take care of the aphids by tickling them with their antennae. Some ants "milk" the aphids inside the colony. The aphids produce honeydew for the ants to feed on. Sometimes the ants chew off their wings.

ANT SURVIVAL FACT

Most ants produce formic acid. It smells bad, which repels predators. Ants will spray formic acid at attackers.

TOP FIVE XTREME ANTS

Xtreme Ant #2

A Bad Reaction Jack jumper ants live in Australia and Tasmania. These ants can jump up to four inches (10.2 cm) when frightened. They are not usually harmful to people. But this species has a stinger that delivers **venom**. Some people are allergic to the venom. They may have to go to the hospital if they are stung. Between 1980 and 2000, four people died from the jack jumper ant's venom!

XCITING FACTS

Ants came from a wasplike insect more than 140 million years ago.

An adult ant does not grow bigger. It will be the same size its entire life.

Dracula ants feed on the blood of their queen's larvae.

The oldest ant fossils ever found were nearly 100 million years old.

Fire ants' nests are large and dense enough to damage farm equipme[nt]

Special foot pads allow weaver ants to carry heavier loads than other ants.

Bulldog ants have superior vision. This helps make them skilled hunters.

Young ants are usually light-colored. They get darker as they grow older.

Fire ant colonies can contain more than 2 million ants!

Soldiers are big and strong. They protect the queen and hunt for f[ood]

Odorous house ants give off a smell like rotten butter.

Giant hunting ant colonies usually contain no more than 12 adults.

A queen carpenter ant can live for up to 25 years.

Ant colonies with mo[re]

Colonies with more than one queen are polygynous.
Colonies with one queen are monogynous.

1

TOP FIVE XTREME ANTS

Xtreme Ant #1

Most Dangerous Ant The bulldog ant is the most dangerous ant in the world. It lives in Australia. Adults are one inch (2.5 cm) long. This ant has strong mandibles. Its bite delivers a powerful venom. It also has a stinger on the end of its abdomen. Bulldog ants bite and sting at the same time. Each bite delivers more and more venom. Since 1931, these ants have killed three people!

GLOSSARY

antennae – body parts that protrude from the head and are used for sensing surroundings

compound eyes – those made up of many parts that see in many directions at once

endangered – in danger of being made extinct, or dying off

honeydew – a sugary liquid expelled from the rear end of aphids and some scale insects

organ – a part of a living being that performs a specific task in the body

venom – poison produced in an animal's body

RESOURCES

"Ant Species of the World." antARK. http://www.antark.net/ant-species.

"Army Ants." Orkin. https://www.insects.orkin.com/entophiles/hymenoptera/army-ants/.

Hölldobler, Bert, and Edward O. Wilson. *The Leafcutter Ants: Civilization by Instinct*. New York: Norton, 2011.

Thaler, Wolfgang. *Ants! Nature's Secret Power*. Directed by Wolfgang Thaler. Germany: ORF Enterprise, 2004.

INDEX

colonies 5, 10, 12, 14, 16, 18, 19, 20, 28, 32

diet 5, 8, 24, 25, 28

drones 19

eggs 12, 16, 19, 20

larvae 12, 16, 22, 28

nests 14, 16, 19, 21, 22, 24, 28

physical features 5, 8, 9, 12, 21, 25, 26, 28, 31

queens 5, 12, 14, 16, 18, 19, 20, 28

soldiers 5, 19, 28

species 5, 6, 7, 8, 9, 10, 12, 16, 19, 20, 21, 22, 24, 25, 26, 28, 31, 32

workers 5, 12, 16, 19, 25

Pavement ant colonies fight each other.

Piles of these ants sometimes appear on sidewalks.